A Little Monster's

GUIDE TO FEELING CALM

A LITTLE MONSTER'S GUIDE TO FEELING CALM

An Hachette UK Company
www.hachette.co.uk

Vie Books, an imprint of Summersdale Publishers
Part of Octopus Publishing Group Limited
Carmelite House
50 Victoria Embankment
LONDON
EC4Y 0DZ
UK

www.summersdale.com

Printed and bound in China

ISBN: 978-1-83799-210-2

Substantial discounts on bulk quantities of Summersdale books are available to corporations, professional associations and other organizations. For details contact general enquiries: telephone: +44 (0) 1243 771107 or email: enquiries@summersdale.com.

A Little Monster's
GUIDE TO FEELING CALM

Emily Snape

Note to parents and carers

This book will help your child to:

- Ease anxiety.

- Recognize their emotions and identify why they are feeling them.

- Learn how to self-regulate and behave constructively in difficult situations.

- Problem-solve for themselves.

The approaches explored in this book can become powerful tools that will encourage your child to manage their feelings and discover inner calm.

Hi!

I'm Cal. It's really grrrreat to meet you.

I'm a LITTLE monster with BIG feelings. Sometimes I get SO cross that I lose my cool and throw a tantrum.

Me in the middle of a tantrum

I've been learning that ALL emotions are important but having tantrums isn't okay. I'm working on ways to manage my feelings and feel calm even when things aren't going my way.

Finding inner calm might seem impossible, especially when your feelings are overwhelming you.

But there are LOTS of ways you can take control of your emotions.

Yesterday, I discovered I could find inner calm and it made me feel so GOOD. I'd love to tell you all about it.

I was SO excited about going to my friend Noodle's birthday party...

Party invitation

Noodle's house, 3 p.m. Saturday

Rock cakes
made with real rocks

Pin the eyeball on the cyclops

Petting zoo with poisonous snakes

Slug smoothies

Vampire disco

But when it was time to go to the party, I couldn't find my stomping boots ANYWHERE and I realized we were going to be late. I was so worried I'd miss out on all the fun, I started to cry.

Grandad suggested I have a sip of water then try the 5-5-5 breathing technique. Here's what you do...

- You breathe in for 5 seconds.
- Then hold your breath for 5 seconds.
- Next, breathe out for 5 seconds.
- Keep doing this until you feel calm.

Afterwards, I felt SOOO much better and that's when I spotted my stomping boots in our pet dragon's drool bowl.

PHEW!

Grandad and I made it to the party in time, but when I was boogieing, Ziggy took my Mr Super Slimy Spider toy and wouldn't give it back.

My whole body suddenly felt HOT and FIZZY. This is because I was angry.

My palms became sticky.

My tail began flicking.

My tummy hurt.

It can be really helpful to recognize how your body feels and try to work out the EMOTION you are experiencing.

Here was my emotion checklist during the party:

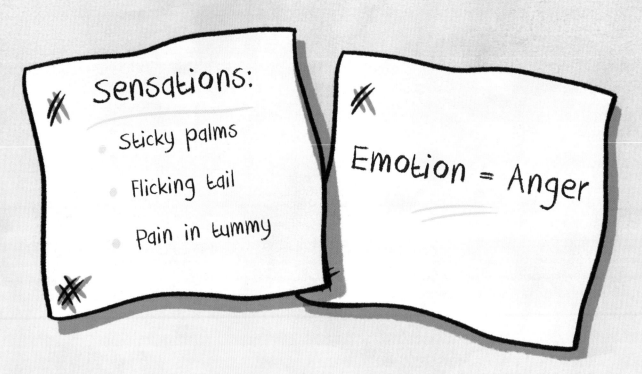

Notice an emotion you are feeling right now and try to rate it on a scale of 1-10.

I wanted to roar, stomp and throw cabbage ice cream at the wall. But that would not have been okay and would not have got my toy back.

Instead, I realized I needed to CALM down so I could work out how to get Mr Super Slimy Spider back.

There are LOTS of ways to discover inner calm when you feel angry.

It can really help to step away from the action and find a quiet space.

I found a peaceful spot in the hallway and tried the 3-3-3 mindfulness technique. Here's what you do:

Name **3** things you can see,

identify **3** things you can hear

and move **3** parts of your body.

The 3-3-3 mindfulness technique can really help you focus on something other than the thing upsetting you so you can relax.

Once I was calm, I could work out how to solve the problem...
I planned to politely ask Ziggy for my toy back.

Guess what? It worked brilliantly! Ziggy handed my toy back and we began playing with it together!

But then, it was time to play Pass the Snot Bag and I lost the game.

Ziggy won and he was given a slug sweet as a prize.

I knew I was losing my cool so I thought about my emotion checklist...

✗ How my body feels:

- Blurry eyesight
- Hands make tight fists
- Spiky feeling in tummy

Scale of 1-10 on the emotion thermometer:

7

Emotion detected:
I was jealous!

After identifying how I felt, and using the 5-5-5 breathing exercise, I was able to calm down and join in with the next activity: Bumps in the Dark.

Guess what? I won a mud splat hat!

Next we were allowed to pet poisonous snakes, and I was having so much fun I accidentally wet myself.

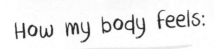
How my body feels:

- Hot cheeks
- Fidgety
- Sinking feeling in tummy

Scale of 1-10 on the emotion thermometer:

10

Emotion detected:
I was embarrassed.

Once I realized I was embarrassed, I felt calmer and was able to ask Grandad for help. He had some spare boots and I went to the bathroom to get changed.

But when I came back into the living room, everything was in total chaos!

One of the baby snakes, Piggles, was missing. With all the panic, there was a chance he might get accidentally stood on and hurt.

Grandad suggested we all tried some calm activities in the garden while the snake keeper searched for Piggles.

These are some of the calm things I like to do:

- Go for a walk
- Lie on the grass and spot clouds
- Have a hug
- Draw a picture
- Listen to soothing music
- Blow bubbles

Do you have any good ideas to add to my list?

Piggles was eventually found and he was fine.

It was time for cake (stinky sock flavour, my favourite) and then it was the end of the party.

I was given a party bag with a cobweb lolly!

On the way home, I talked with Grandad about each time I had lost my cool and how I had solved each problem calmly.

He explained it can be helpful to role play the times I might throw a tantrum to practise managing my emotions.

He said to remember that hitting and throwing things in anger is never okay.

The party had been SO much fun and Grandad even said I could invite Ziggy over to play the next day.

My head was bursting with all the ideas of what we could do together and fizzing with everything that had happened at the party that I didn't feel like I would ever get to sleep.

While I felt like doing cartwheels, Grandad said it is really important to go to bed at a regular time each day and to get enough sleep to be healthy.

Here are Grandad's tips on how to calm down at bedtime (and they really work!):

→ Avoid screens before bedtime

→ Listen to soothing music or an audio book

→ Don't be too hot or cold

→ Take deep breaths

→ Visualize a peaceful setting – I like to imagine a slime swimming pool

Wow! What a day!

It wasn't easy, but I am so proud that
I was able to manage my emotions.

I've discovered being calm puts you in a
positive mood, helps you problem solve
and feels grrreat.

I can't wait for Ziggy to come over.
I have so many calm activities planned!

About the Author

Emily Snape is a children's author and illustrator living in London. Her work has appeared online, on television, in shops and even on buses! She loves coffee and notebooks, and has three cheeky children, Leo, Fin and Flo, who keep her on her toes and give her lots of inspiration for stories.

You can find out her latest publishing news on Instagram at **@emily_snape_illustrator**.

If you're interested in finding out
more about our books, find us on Facebook
at **Summersdale Publishers**, on Twitter/X
at **@Summersdale** and on Instagram and TikTok
at **@summersdalebooks** and get in touch.

We'd love to hear from you!

Thanks very much for buying
this Summersdale book.

www.summersdale.com